Timekeeping

Alan Tomkins

Amateur Athletic Association

The Crowood Press

First published in 1987 by
The Crowood Press
Ramsbury, Marlborough,
Wiltshire, SN8 2HE

British Library Cataloguing in Publication Data
Tomkins, Alan
Timekeeping.
1. Track-athletics   2. Timekeeping
I. Title
798.4'26   GV1060.67

ISBN 1 85223 027 4

Picture Credits
Fig 5 is by Hird-Smith Timing Ltd; Fig 6 is
by Racecourse Technical Services

Typeset by Lee Typesetting, Warminster
Printed in Great Britain

Contents

Preface

The notes on timekeeping first published in 1963 and reprinted in 1977 now need revision because of minor changes in the rules and the replacement of 'ticking' watches by digital read-out electronic timers. The original text by the late H.A. Hathway was part of a booklet *The Technique of Starting and Timekeeping* and so dealt mainly with technique – the skill and proficiency required, and methods of practice to acquire these – before going on to the application of technique by a Timekeeper at sports meetings. Amendments to the 1977 edition were issued in 1981, noting minor rule changes as well as laying more emphasis on the duties of a Chief Timekeeper, because such knowledge is now needed for advancement to the higher grades.

The sport is much indebted to the late Harry Hathway for his dedication to timekeeping and his devotion to the achievement of accuracy. His plan for the 'Timekeepers' Practical Test' has indeed stood the test of time, for it has remained unaltered, apart from a minor change in the marking scale in order to maintain the earlier standards now that most candidates use hundredths of a second timers. With more frequent opportunities for comparing timings against photo-finish results, and the general use of electronic timers with their negligible starting and stopping errors, standards of accuracy have significantly improved and British timekeeping is respected, and envied, by the rest of the world.

Thanks are due to so many colleagues that I cannot mention them all by name here – I have merely tried to assemble their combined wisdom. Those asked to comment on the draft copy made many useful suggestions which I have gratefully incorporated. Some relevant topics, although not necessarily required knowledge for the Written Paper, are noted in the Appendices.

The original notes, with the current Handbook, were prescribed reading for candidates taking Timekeepers' Written Tests, and it is hoped that this booklet will be found useful too.

Introduction

Good timekeeping is required in athletics for establishing records, for assessing qualifying times, for seeding and team selection, as well as for the gratification of competitors achieving personal best performances. 'Winning' is directly influenced by timekeeping in the time-trials of combined events (decathlons etc.) and by the selection of fastest losers when timings decide the composition of subsequent rounds of the competition. For those taking part and seeking personal bests, timekeeping needs to be reliably accurate in fairness to athletes. Although at major meetings photo-finish timing will be used, there are exceptions, and Timekeepers should strive to attain accuracy comparable with electronic timing.

The purpose of this booklet is to interest potential Timekeepers in the techniques of timekeeping and the equipment used, to suggest how more accurate timings may be achieved, to help candidates in examinations for grading, and to consider timekeeping at major meetings, where you may be in charge of the timekeeping team. Appendices note topics which may be of interest but are *not* required for the Written Test Papers.

Grading depends mainly on practice and experience; the Grading Scheme is described in the Handbook section 'Testing and Grading of Officials' which should be consulted.

For the Preliminary Written Test Paper, which is a simple test to ensure that the candidate has read and, hopefully, understood the relevant rules, the topics in Chapters 1 to 3 aim to cover the syllabus, but the other sections should also be of interest. For the Advanced Written Paper, which is set to assess a candidate's approach to problems in practice, as well as his detailed knowledge of the rules relating to timekeeping, Chapters 4 to 6 provide the skeleton information, but the flesh can only be added by experience gained at major meetings. A Practical Test is also required for grading, and the notes on it in Chapter 3 may be useful. Appendix III has further details.

1
Equipment, Technique and Practice

WATCHES AND TIMERS

It is generally assumed in this booklet that Timekeepers will be using digital read-out quartz-controlled electronic timers, hereafter called 'electronic timers', but references to mechanical 'ticking' watches are included for comparison. The rules cover both types, allowing 'any manually operated timing device' (note at the head of Rule 40). The terms 'timer' and 'watch' are now tending to distinguish between the two types.

Electronic timers have important advantages over conventional ticking watches. They are more accurate, their starting and stopping errors are so small that they may be ignored, their readings are unambiguous (there is no stopping of a hand between dial divisions), there are not wear problems because there are no moving parts except in operating switches so no servicing is required, and they are more tolerant of misuse than conventional watches. However, they do tend to be more easily harmed by damp. Because of their better long-period accuracy and negligible starting and stopping errors, the rules allow that *one* electronic timer can replace the three conventional watches that dedicated Timekeepers previously found it necessary to own and maintain. The 'split' function provided by the costlier mechanical watches is matched in the cheaper electronic timers (although one time may be lost when the second is displayed), and is surpassed in the slightly more costly ones with micro-chip memories that can store several timings for recall when required. Models with paper print-out are available at extra cost.

Second-hand watches may be tempting, but unless their complete history is known, it is doubtful whether they are worth buying. Even if their history is known and fully documented, and the offer is a bargain, it should be remembered that servicing and recertification (Rule 40) will be costly; each three-yearly outlay would buy a new electronic timer. Soon, the services of horologists with the necessary skills will be harder to find, and those treasured 'tickers' will have become museum pieces.

TECHNIQUE AND PRACTICE

Timekeeping is simple: it is merely to determine the interval between the start and finish of a race. Timekeepers, like all other officials, must be people of integrity, they should have adequate vision (the Starter's pistol must be seen clearly from 150m or so away from half-lap starts) and in particular should have the ability to concentrate, hard, for the few moments at the start and finish of races. While they are part of the timekeeping team, they must be for those moments, egoists, as they have to work on their own – 'time independently', as the rules state.

Hints on operating a ticking watch were easily summarised: hold the watch firmly, but not in too tense a manner with nerves all at tingling point; use the inside of the top joint of a fore-finger to operate the push-pieces with as little lost motion as possible; find a method that suits you, and practise with it.

Modern electronic timers vary so much in the disposition and type of their push-pieces that the only phrase of current value in the above is the final one, that is, find a method that suits *you* and practise with it. However, hints from the earlier days can be useful: hold the timer firmly but in a relaxed manner, avoiding excessive tenseness, and for push-piece operation use a part of a finger with little flesh, for example the inside of a joint, or a finger end. The soft, fleshy pads of thumbs or fingers only introduce lost motion. Timing is generally a two-handed operation, holding the timer in one hand and using the fingers of the other to operate the push-pieces. Experienced colleagues will not be impressed if you have a timer in each hand, or indulge in theatrical gestures as if the timer was being snatched from space or flung into it.

It is important to get the 'feel' of a new timer. Having one that suits you, find the best way of holding and operating it, then practise with it: stop and start and split while watching traffic in the road come to some landmark; time track-side signs during a railway journey, indeed, do anything that will make the operations familiar to you. Consistency of reaction and operation are essential to good timekeeping.

Practice at actual meetings is the best practice of all, but some private practice can be done at home and some assessment made of your competence and consistency. Three schemes are detailed in Appendix I, to which reference should be made. All these methods for 'at home' checks on your timekeeping are useful for improving consistency and, moreover, are convincing proof that your reactions are not that fast after all!

It does indeed take 1½ to 2 or more tenths of a second for a finger to respond to a visual signal. Such practice will also give a useful check on the consistency of reaction times – a series of around 0.17–0.20 seconds is more useful than the odd 0.15 and some 0.22s. That difference would represent significant errors at starts and finishes of races. If your reaction times vary from 0.15 to 0.20 seconds and at the start of a particular race you achieve 0.15 seconds delay and at the finish a 0.20 seconds delay, your timing for this race will be 0.05 seconds 'slow'. On the other hand, if your reaction time at the start is 0.20 seconds and at the finish 0.15 seconds, your timing will be 0.05 seconds 'fast'. Home exercises with pendulum and 'dart', or covered timer, are useful preparation for the actual job of timing at meetings, their object being the attainment of consistency which is the factor of greatest value in good timekeeping. Practice can help achieve that. Reasons for the in-built delay are suggested in Appendix II.

Quite the best practice, of course, is with experienced Timekeepers at actual meetings. Novice Timekeepers can ask the Chief Timekeeper before the meeting if they may join the timekeeping team. This is so much better than standing with the spectators, often off the finish line, and grumbling that 'they've got it slow again!'. Chiefs are usually approachable and welcome offers of assistance from anyone interested in timekeeping; they will usually put the newcomer to work with some experienced team member, who will be able to give good advice on technique. A novice showing promise may be invited to other meetings, for there are rarely too many Timekeepers.

2
At the Meeting

Assume that you have been invited to timekeep at your first meeting – perhaps a League fixture or a County Championships. You should arrive in good time before the first race (at least half an hour early), and report to the organisers of the meeting and to the Chief Timekeeper, who cannot complete his duty allocation until he is sure that all members of the team are present.

While in the current Preliminary Written Test Papers details of the allocation of duties are not question topics as they were previously, knowledge of them may help in appreciating the Chief's problems. The Chief will ask you to time one or, perhaps, two placings, and you should make sure that you clearly understand the instructions. For example, if you are asked to time thirds in sprints, does this include 400m? You should *never* be asked to time more than one placing in sprint events. The Chief will probably assume that you know the basic rules, but if you have *any* doubts regarding your duties, ask – the Chief will advise you, for he too had the same problems a few years earlier. You must, of course, as Rule 40 requires, 'time independently' and show your watch (or tell your time) to the Chief Timekeeper 'immediately after the race'. It is the Chief's job to 'agree the times', and for the Written Paper you must know the principles on which his decision is based: all three times different – the middle time is taken; two the same, one different – the two; only two times – the longer. If you are using a ticking watch you must be careful to report the time to the next longer dial division if the hand happens to stop between divisions. Using a watch or timer reading in hundredths, any time not ending in zero will be returned to the 'next tenth' as required in the rules, for example 10.11 will be read as 10.2. In the Written Test it must be remembered that a 'hand' time reading of 10.00 is returned as 10.0; candidates often seem hypnotised by the zeros and write a mark-losing 10.00. *All 'hand' times are returned in tenths, never in hundredths* – it may look clever, but knowledgeable people will know that it is merely foolish, so keep the hundredths to yourself, to check against photo-finish timings if the opportunity occurs.

In Rule 40 there is an escape clause for Chief Timekeepers regarding 'agreed times'. The phrase is 'unless he is satisfied that a mistake has been made'. For example, a timekeeping team for a particular place in a 200m may return 21.2, 21.3, and 21.0. However, this last runner finished about half a metre behind one timed at 21.2, 21.2 and 21.3 by another team. Obviously the 21.0 was a mistake, and so the Chief would ignore it and, with then only two times, would take the longer of these, 21.3.

Imagine that you are about to time real races at your first meeting, working with Timekeepers with more experience than yourself. It would be unusual if you did not feel a bit tense for your first few timings. However, the Chief and your experienced colleagues will understand this, sympathise, and make allowances, for they once felt the same.

The Chief will have asked you to time a particular placing, or, in longer events if you have a split timer, two placings. So to the job itself: it is simply to determine as accurately as you can the interval between the start and finish of a race. Therefore we need to define 'start' and 'finish', as well as to consider what we have to do and how best to do it.

THE START

The *start* is defined in the Handbook, Rule 30 – the start *line* is of no real concern to Timekeepers. To the runners, the start is the report from the pistol; to Timekeepers it is the *flash* from the pistol. The reason for this is that sound travels slowly, light very quickly. Sound travels at about 330 metres per second, varying a little with temperature etc. Therefore, in the ten metres or so from the Starter to the runners, there will be a delay of about a thirtieth of a second – accepted as part of the race. However, in a 100 metre event the Timekeepers will be 100 metres or more from the Starter, and the sound from the gun will take about a third of a second to reach them – *not* accepted as part of the race. Light travels this distance in a few millionths of a second, so this is the signal we use. If Timekeepers waited for the sound to reach them, their 100m times would be over 0.3 seconds fast! Hence Rule 30: 'The time will be taken from the flash'.

For the start, the Timekeepers must be able to see the Starter's pistol clearly when it is raised for firing: Rule 30 also requires that 'it should give a satisfactory flash'. To have a clear line of sight to the Starter, an elevated stand is required. You must also be able to see the finish, so this defines the position of the stand: in line with the finish and with a clear view of the Starter. It is usual for the Starters to wear red jackets and for the one actually starting the race to wear a red cap. Other members of the starting team should be hatless.

When the runners are preparing to start their race, the Starter whistles to the Chief Timekeeper who, having ascertained that his team are ready (and also having checked that the Referee and Judges are ready) waves to the Starter – a flag is useful for easy recognition among a crowd. While this is being done, the Time-keepers should check that their timers have been returned to zero – it saves embarrassment later. The Starter acknowledges this signal and prepares for the start. From then until the race is started, the Timekeepers must not take their attention from the Starter, and when the actual race is imminent and the pistol raised for firing, they must concentrate their vision *only on the pistol barrel*. Visual acuity is highest over a *very* small angle, not much larger than the size of a pistol at a distance of 100 metres. *Movement* can be detected over a wider angle but don't make this an excuse to see who 'beat the gun'. Timekeepers are not concerned with the movements: they must see nothing but the pistol. Good Starters will ensure that the pistol is held steady after calling 'set' – movement of the pistol is bad for the con-centration of Timekeepers.

At the instant the flash appears at the pistol muzzle you '*start* to start' the watch by depressing the appropriate button. Note that you will '*start* to start' it, for we know that it takes about 0.2 seconds to start a watch from a distant visual signal. This varies with individuals, of course, and also with the degree of stimulus, for we react a little more quickly to a strong stimulus than to a weak one. For example, a poor flash at a 200m start gets slower reactions than a good flash at a 400m start. In the latter, the report from the pistol is not too delayed, and it is well established that two good stimuli are better than one. The physiologists have these effects well documented (*see* Appendix II). Incidentally, the runners themselves, with the relatively strong stimulus from a pistol report near them, take nearly the same length of time as the Timekeepers to react, but this is accepted as part of the race.

You have started the timer. If you have been concentrating hard, you may naturally still be tense, and it is good practice to relax, that is, to let your arms and hands go limp, and just watch the race. In sprints you will not have very long to do this, but even a few seconds relaxation seems useful. If, for any reason, the watch fails to start, you should inform the Chief Timekeeper *immediately* so that he can ensure that the placing is covered.

THE FINISH

The *finish* is defined as a line 5cm wide across the track at right angles to the inner edge, and the 'finish plane', with which Time-keepers are concerned, is vertically above the edge of the finish line nearer the start. Timekeepers should not be too near the runners – six metres is a *minimum*. Ten, twenty or more metres from the runners is even better because the angular speed is thereby reduced across your field of view. Judges need to be nearer to the runners than Timekeepers do, for they have to be able to distinguish the competitors' numbers quickly. If Judges and Timekeepers work from the same side of the track, the Judges will usually prefer to be in front of the Timekeepers.

The elevated stand that the Timekeepers use to have a clear view of the Starter must be arranged so that they are aligned with the finish plane. White worsted stretched between posts outside the track may be used at the finish as a guide to com-petitors but is useless to Timekeepers. The far post, however, is useful – with the edge of the finish line – to denote the plane of the finish so this post must be properly aligned. To 'break the tape' is not to win; it may be blown out of alignment.

When the runners are about ten metres from the finish it is time to make ready for the next phase of the timekeeping task. From that time, do not watch the runners, watch only the plane of the finish. In practice, you concentrate on the far post along the edge of the finish line nearer the start. When the torso of the runner you are timing (the winner is easiest) reaches the plane of the finish, 'start to stop' the timer. Note the *start* to stop; you will probably feel the 'click' when the runner is well past the post if you started to stop the timer when you saw the torso at the finish plane. Your timer should have recorded the correct time interval.

Different signals operate at the start and finish. At the start, without warning, we had the sudden appearance of the flash from the Starter's pistol – we could not anticipate its appearance. But at the finish, things are very different. We can see the runners approaching, and we can easily, and subconsciously perhaps, estimate the moment when the torso will reach the finish plane, and so have the timer stopped at that instant. The time will be wrong – fast by about 0.2 seconds, which was the delay interval that our physiology incurred for us at the start. Quite the most common error of novice Timekeepers is anticipation, always the result of watching the runners come to the finish.

As Rule 32 states, the placings – and times – are determined by the torso reaching the plane of the finish. Torso is defined as the *body*, as distinguished from the neck, head, arms, legs, hands or feet. Remember that there are six 'loose ends' listed! If you started to start the timer as soon as possible after you saw the flash from the Starter's pistol, and started to stop it at the instant the torso reached the finish plane, you will have the correct time interval.

Without consulting your colleagues, you will report the time to the Chief Timekeeper when he asks for it; he may, if he needs confirmation, ask to see the time recorded; indeed, he *must* see the timers if records are involved. When the Chief is satisfied, the timer should be returned to zero in readiness for the next race.

INTERNATIONAL MEETINGS

At international meetings, the times have to be entered on a Timekeepers' Record Form, signed and handed to the Chief Timekeeper as the IAAF Rules require. It is usual for the Chief Timekeeper at 'Internationals' to ask for hundredths of seconds to be entered on the Timekeepers' Record Forms to assist him in deciding the agreed timings (in tenths), for in very close finishes deciding just where a change of tenth is appropriate requires the exercise of judgement. To have a tenth of a second between runners finishing only centimetres apart looks inept, whatever the photo-finish timings may reveal later. In these situations the Chief has to rely on judgement, experience, and luck. With a *very* good team working in ideal conditions (for example, with good flash etc.) the arithmetical average of a sub-team's hundredths may provide useful hints. Appendix V has some examples of this. Such problems make timekeeping at this level the fascinating study that it is.

DUTIES

Timekeeping at meetings is a team function, your team leader being the Chief Timekeeper for the meeting. He will ask you to undertake certain duties, and your responsibilities are solely to him. The Chief will probably know your capabilities if you live locally; if not, he will need to know your Grade to guide him in allocating duties for his team. Waiting for all his team members to report is an axious time for the Chief Timekeeper. You must therefore report to him as soon as you arrive at the stadium; half an hour before the first track event is not too early. When the Chief has checked his team, he will, at local meetings, probably give you verbal instructions; at larger meetings he may give you an Instruction Card. The range of possible tasks you will know from the rules, and one or more of the following will be included:

1. Take times for *one* placing in sprints (or races in lanes).
2. Take times for two finishers in longer races, that is, those

not in lanes. You may be asked to report your time to one of the team timing your placing as a sub-team reporter. He will make a preliminary agreement on the time and report to the Chief Time-keeper. If there seem to be problems, the Chief may ask to see the timers so do not 'zero' until you are given permission. This procedure is often adopted at busy meetings to save time, which not only aids presentation but also assists the photo-finish team.

3.   Record lap times – important if records are likely. An IAAF safeguard (IAAF Rule 123) requires lap scoring to be supplemented by lap timing for each competitor in races of over 5,000m. With the restricted fields usual in major international meetings, this is rarely applied, but with larger fields (perhaps thirty or more runners) it is the only safe way by which the Referee can confirm that each finisher has completed the distance. The arrangements and system employed are the responsibility of the Referee, who may ask that the Chief Time-keeper provides Timekeepers for his lap scorers. In practice, however, one Timekeeper with a loud voice (or better, a loud-hailer) stands at the finish line and calls times, to the next second from a running watch, as competitors complete each lap. The Referee's team of Recorders each write down these times on a lap/time chart for the runners (usually three or four) for whom the Referee has made them responsible. The more usual lap scoring procedure, which is not timed, is described in the AAA booklet *How to Judge Track Events*.

4.   Call lap times to the runners – generally at the finish line, but in the quarter or half-lap starts a caller may be required at those points as well. Lap calling can be of great help to com-petitors aiming for records or personal bests but it must be done properly to be effective – at one to two metres past the finish line to avoid interference with the Judges or with the runners' view of a lap time clock. Call in a loud clear voice directed at the runners' ears, not mumbled down to their feet. The Caller should aim to be calling the *seconds* as each runner comes to him; the minutes are less important, even if there is time to say them. Usually the lap indicator board and the bell to signal the start of the final lap will be a couple of metres before the finish line, and if the Caller starts to announce the minutes as the runner passes it, the seconds will be voiced as the runner comes

to him; this may however need adjustment to suit the pace of the event. A word with the ringer of the bell asking for the ring to be finished before the runners get to you for the final lap should ensure that the times called are heard effectively.

Note that no lap times (or any other intermediate times) may be called or indicated to competitors except by an Official Timekeeper appointed to do so (Rules 31 and 40).

5.   Take kilometre times in races of 3,000m and over – usually a sub-team of Timekeepers will do this for the leading runners. Note that the kilometres come at full and half-laps alternately on standard 400m tracks, but in steeplechases and at non-standard tracks they are at odd positions. A well-appointed stadium will have these positions marked on the track and small but distinctive flags will be placed there.

6.   Take split times for team members in relay races (but *never* in 4 × 100m or 4 × 200m races). Times are taken as the *baton* crosses the finish plane, but note that the first take-over when staggered starts are used is not at the finish line, except for runners in the inside lane. The Chief will advise you if you are in doubt about the take-over positions for your team.

7.   Do a 'running watch'. The timer is started as usual on seeing the flash from the gun and as each runner finishes, the time (to the next whole second) is called to a Recorder who notes it down. The only problem likely to arise is from lapped runners. The best safeguard is to keep a Lap Scoring Chart (as Judges do), but in a simplified form, that is, neglecting individuals in close groups in the early stages. If in doubt, check when the bell is given to runners for their final lap. In large fields, when individual times from stopped watches are unlikely to be possible for the later finishers, those from a running watch are a useful record as well as a check on earlier finishers' times. Electronic timers with multiple memories or print-outs are useful here, the timer being 'split' as each runner finishes.

8.   Standards Timekeeping. This is required now only at club or schools' meetings, when there are time standards to be equalled or bettered for some events, for example a fifth-year 1500m Standard may be 4 minutes 40 seconds. Having started the watch from the flash signal from the Starter's gun, the Standards Timekeeper goes with a Judge (appointed by the Referee) to the

finish line. As the runners come to the finish, the Judge counts them until the Timekeeper announces the completion of the Standard Time. This he does by calling 'up' and/or tapping the Judge on the shoulder. Sometimes there may be more than one Standard Time, for example fourth, fifth, and sixth year Standards; in this case, it is helpful to jot these down on a card before going with your Judge to the finish line.

Another ancillary piece of information needed by Timekeepers concerns fastest losers; there are invariably questions on this in the Preliminary Written Test Paper. A fastest loser is a competitor who goes forward to the next round on *time*, not on placing. Note that the second in the heat in which the winner did the fastest time is not necessarily the fastest loser; he may be, but it depends on his time. Usually in the Written Test, a table is given of times and placings in a number of heats and the qualifying conditions are also given, for example: 'the first two in each heat and two fastest losers compete in the semi-final'. The heat winners and seconds go to the next round on placing qualification, and all you have to do is to find the two fastest competitors from the remainder. Note that both may be in one heat. It would not be a fair question in the Preliminary Written Test Paper, but if, by chance, there are more fastest losers than required, the problem must be resolved by the Referee. He should arrange for an additional round to the competition – a run-off – or put extra runners in the next round. The problem is his, not the Timekeepers'.

Races partly or entirely outside the track, such as Marathons, are timed to the next whole second by splitting or, if the finishers are too close for this, by calling from a running watch. A good recorder is a 'must'. Note that there are no 'records' as such for these events, only best performances. At events with very large numbers of competitors (for example, a National Cross Country Championship) runners sometimes finish in such large bunches that even calling from a running watch may not be possible. The preferred procedure is to time a competitor *and note his number* at convenient intervals (perhaps five to ten seconds) until the situation eases and one can revert to a running or split watch reading (the Judges have the correct finishing order and a time here and there is better than no time at all for a longer period). Such questions on large numbers in races are not in the Preliminary Written Test Paper.

In combined events (decathlon, for example) the rules require 'at least two Timekeepers' for every competitor. It is safer, if numbers permit, to use the normal complement of three Timekeepers timing independently, especially if records may be involved. Note that only if photo-finish timing is operating can hundredths of seconds be used, and this requires photo-finish timings for *all* the track events. If there should be some malfunction resulting in no, or suspect, timings for one track event, then hand timings (to tenths of seconds) have to be used for the whole competition.

ERRORS: CAUSES AND REMEDIES

During practical timekeeping at meetings working with more experienced Timekeepers, the novice may notice that his timings are sometimes different from those of his colleagues, and if photo-finish equipment is in use, from this electronic timing as well. Questioning the causes of these discrepancies is the best way to improve your timekeeping. It may be useful to group the errors and suggest their likely causes.

Fast times are usually due to:

1. Anticipation at the finish. Avoid this by *not* watching the runners over the final few metres; watch *only* the far post.
2. Time lost at the start, due to inattention, a poor gun signal, or a poor view of the start.
3. Timing the wrong runner.
4. Neglecting to round up to the next tenth of a second.
5. Inexperience.
6. Watch errors (unlikely with electronic timers).

Slow times – rarer – are usually due to:

1. Inattention at the finish, being distracted by the crowd, for example.

2.   Timing the wrong runner.
3.   Starting error, due to excessive tenseness or, rarely, the Starter failing to hold the gun steady.
4.   Inexperience.
5.   Watch errors (unlikely with electronic timers).

Inconsistent times are usually due to:

1.   Excessive tenseness – minimised with more experience.
2.   Inexperience.
3.   Timing wrong numbers.
4.   Attempting to take two times with runners finishing too close together.
5.   Distraction. Sometimes people may move into your line of sight. To shout at the offender is unseemly and may distract colleagues. Do your best calmly to ignore the disturbance.
6.   Watch errors (unlikely with electronic timers).

It may well be asked how accurate hand timings are? Well-practised, higher-graded Timekeepers achieve timings surprisingly close – usually within a few hundredths – to those of the photo-finish, which can be taken as correct unless some system fault gives a 'nonsense' time. Appendix V gives typical figures and a simple method for assessing personal performances.

From the above will be seen ways in which errors may be minimised: get a good view of the start and finish, avoid being too tense, maintain concentration and time independently. At the start of races, see, hear and be aware of nothing but the Starter's gun and, at the finish, the runner you are to time coming to the far post. You will get the right time; the others may be wrong.

3
Grading and Examinations

To become graded, that is a qualified Timekeeper, and therefore to be accepted by national and international organisations, there is an established Grading Scheme. For details of this, see the current Handbook, *The Testing and Grading of Officials*, which notes the syllabus and the Practical Test. Grading is especially important for Timekeepers as it gives authenticity to times, from personal bests in the village school sports, to qualifying times for the Olympic Games. Timekeepers are urged to take these tests, which are not too daunting.

The syllabus for the Written Papers, outlined in the Handbook, is covered in this booklet, and it may be useful to mention the procedure for the Practical Test in which candidates are required to time the leading runner in forty sprint races. The candidates' times are compared with those obtained by an experienced Timekeeper who has been appointed as the Master by the Area. Care is taken that the candidates can give their best performances by having conditions as ideal as possible, for example good whistle and gun signals, good view of the start and finish, and as few distractions as possible (or that race is ignored). A good Master will ensure that candidates are put, and kept, at their ease during what can naturally be a trying time. Times are written down, not spoken aloud, in case this should give other candidates cause for concern that, if their times differ, they may be wrong (if they are slower, they are probably right!). The Master and most of the candidates use timers reading in hundredths, and the marking scheme, based on the original one from the 1950s, marks as 'correct' those timings by candidates within ten 'hundredths' of the Master's timings. Most candidates who have had a little timekeeping experience (but a lot of pendulum practice), usually get 70 per cent to 80 per cent or more; after a season's practical experience, 80 per cent to 90 per cent and over is generally achieved. Appendix III has notes on the Practical Test.

The Practical Test may be taken before or after the Written Paper. A 70 per cent Practical mark is required to merit Grade IV (Probationary). A mark for the Preliminary Written Paper over 65 per cent (the pass mark) with 70 per cent or more in the Practical Test and a year's practical experience would enable the County or Service (District for the NCAA) to award suitably experienced Timekeepers a Grade III. Requirements for the other gradings are given in the AAA Handbook. The emphasis on experience should be noted as a requirement for the higher gradings, as well as the higher standard of timekeeping.

After passing the Timekeepers' Preliminary Written Paper, getting 90 per cent or over in the Practical Test, and acquiring the necessary experience to have achieved the status of Grade II, Timekeepers may be invited by their Area or Service to take the Advanced Written Paper, for which the Pass Mark is 75 per cent. The syllabus for this Advanced Paper is based almost entirely on experience at major meetings, so the printed word or lecture is no substitute for practical experience with timekeeping teams at major events, which candidates will be encouraged to attend. The following chapters attempt to cover likely questions.

4

Chief Timekeeper's Duties

Chief Timekeepers are not just better-than-average Grade I Timekeepers. Their duties, besides getting the correct times for each runner in accordance with the Rules for Competition and dealing with possible discrepancies and problems, cover a much wider field, embracing not only national rules but international ones too. Chief Timekeepers must be able to make wise decisions quickly and authoritatively, to be diplomatic with enquirers from the Jury of Appeal to the media, to co-operate quickly and effectively with other officials such as the Track Referee, Photo-finish Chief, Meeting Director and others. Generally they must have personal attributes that could be regarded as 'leadership'. Chief Timekeepers will therefore be thoroughly conversant with National and International Rules, and study of current Rule Books is essential for the Advanced Written Paper. IAAF Rules, published every two years, are available from the International Amateur Athletic Federation, 3 Hans Crescent, Knightsbridge, London, SW1X 0LN.

An important part of the Chief Timekeeper's task, fore-stalling possible difficulties later, is done a few days before the meeting, and relates to the arrangement of the team's duties. In order that these can be organised to the best advantage, the Meeting Secretary must send a programme (or at least Time-keepers' acceptances and a timed list of events) to the Chief Timekeeper a few days before the meeting so that all the timekeeping requirements, for example functions like splits in relays can be considered. A note of any Timekeepers who may have accepted the engagement but who, due to unforeseen circumstances, cannot be present is most helpful – even up to the day before the meeting – so that any rearrangement of the team can be given due thought. A telephone message even an hour or two before the meeting can prevent last-minute problems.

The Secretary of the Meeting should advise each Timekeeper, well before the date of the event, of the programme times, preferred dress and, where required, such details as accommodation, routes to the venue, car parking facilities etc. Generally he or she will act as host to visitors. It may save travel expense if other Officials' names and addresses are sent so that mutual travel arrangements may be made.

Being in charge of a timekeeping team at prestige meetings needs some careful preparatory work which differs in details for national and international meetings.

NATIONAL MEETINGS

Ideally twenty-four Timekeepers should be used at important meetings, three timing each runner in sprint races with eight competitors. Given sufficient Timekeepers, arranging the team for sprints is fairly easy, and with a full complement it is useful to appoint one of each sub-team of three to agree the times and report for his colleagues. He should also keep a note of the times recorded, so that only in cases of doubt or possible records will the Chief Timekeeper himself need to check the watch times.

Team arrangements for the longer distances are generally easier and with twenty or more Timekeepers, each with split watches taking two timings each, there will be sufficient for the later finishers to be timed, as well as for extra duties like lap-calling and splitting, giving lap times to the Announcers, having a running watch as a check in the longer events etc.

In making out the team arrangement, the Chief will use any known attributes of his team as well as noting differences in ability within grades; for example, a very good Grade II may be as good as a poor Grade I, and while the experienced Chief will know these distinctions within the grades among colleagues in his own locality, he will find it an advantage to contact experienced Timekeepers often working in the district in which the meeting is to take place. Information on the lesser-known team members can then be obtained so that any special skills can be properly employed, and any disabilities allowed for. For example, a good Timekeeper but a bad stutterer would not be asked to call lap times to the runners. Such niceties have no part in Written Test questions; various grades are assumed taking no account of differences within the grades or of special attributes. Team arrangement for the Advanced Written Test is discussed later.

At an unfamiliar venue, it is advisable to check that there is a clear route to one side of the Timekeepers' rows of seating, and preferably to both sides. If not, this should be arranged.

INTERNATIONAL MEETINGS

Chief Timekeepers' duties are much the same as at national meetings, but they are required to be conversant with the IAAF Rules regarding timekeeping, under which (IAAF Rule 119): 'Each Timekeeper shall act independently and, without showing his watch to, or discussing his time with any other person, enter his time on the printed form, and after signing the form, hand it to the Chief Timekeeper, who may examine watches to verify the reported times.' Forms are required and should be provided by the organisers of the meeting.

Timekeeper's Result Slip

Event	
Place	Time
Timekeeper	

Fig 1   The layout of a typical Timekeeper's result slip.

It is helpful, with IAAF requirements to be met, to appoint a Chief Timekeeper's Clerk to help collect the forms and generally to do the office work, thus leaving the Chief free to give full attention to the job in hand, that is, to see that the timekeeping is in strict accordance with the IAAF Rules. It may seem that the Chief at an International could be too busy to take times himself, but IAAF Rule 119 requires that he and two other Timekeepers time the winner. For the Chief to be too concerned with 'office work' is not using a good Timekeeper to best advantage; it also contravenes the Rules. The appointment of a Chief Timekeeper's Clerk is almost a 'must'.

There are other important differences from national meeting requirements:

1. 'Additional' Timekeepers must be provided; their duty is to start a watch for each race and be prepared to time any placing at the Chief Timekeeper's request.
2. Timekeepers' Result Slips must be used, and signed (or a reference letter appended), but in the case of a record they *must be signed*.
3. At major meetings where photo-finish cameras are in use, the time recorded is the 'fully automatic timing' of IAAF Rule 120 – which must be studied and applied. These times are official unless it is agreed that they are obviously inaccurate, when hand timings (to tenths of seconds) become official.
4. For races exceeding 5,000m, and for walking events, the Referee may ask that official Timekeepers give times to his appointed Lap Scorers.

Collection of results forms is facilitated if seating positions are allocated. If a reference number or letter is used, this can be put on the Timekeeper's Record Form; this saves having to decipher signatures and is recommended. It is useful, too, if subsequent to the meeting the Chief issues a record of the team's performances compared with the photo-finish times. The reference letters used above may save embarrassment (*see* Appendix V, for interest, *not* for the Written Test).

A better overall picture of the race finish is obtained from an elevated position and it seems preferable for the Chief Timekeeper to be at the top of the row of seats allocated to the Timekeeping team. It is easier to 'read the race' from above, and there are likely to be fewer enthusiastic media men interfering with your view of the finish. However, another requirement is ease of communication, and this may warrant some sacrifice of elevation – or involve a lot of walking up and down steps. These arrangements will be made known at a pre-meeting discussion.

BEFORE THE MEETING

The usual practice is to hold a Technical Committee before an international meeting, and the Chief Timekeeper should attend this so that questions such as communication routes to the Photo-finish team, Referee, Announcers and others can be considered. The Committee also presents an opportunity for the Chief to arrange 'readiness' signals with the Starter and Referee, and to establish liaison with the meeting's main Officials.

The conclusions of the Technical Committee, as they affect Timekeepers, are conveyed to the team at a Briefing Meeting, generally on the day of the meeting, an hour or so before the start of the competition. Such a meeting provides an opportunity for the Chief to meet the team, to pass on his instructions and to resolve any difficulties that may be foreseen. It is the final chance to check that all the team members are present, and to take the necessary action to cover for any absentees. Spare additional Timekeepers can cover such contingencies.

Sometimes the Meeting Organisers will want Officials to march on to the arena, such arrangements having been decided at the Technical Committee. The Briefing Meeting will provide the opportunity to arrange this. For instance, the Chief Timekeeper would normally be expected to lead on his team, and any ladies would follow next, in front of the gentlemen. If one of the team has any experience in the services, it is useful to let him 'size' the team as an aid to better presentation. A few of the team may not wish to march. They can be asked to take bags and other impedimenta surreptitiously (for example, through the stand) to the Timekeepers' seating, and stay with them, leaving the marchers only the permitted programme etc., to carry. The Chief will not be impressed by too many sudden attacks of lameness, for the knowledgeable public will expect to see enough Timekeepers to do the job properly.

Prior to the meeting, it is useful to find out from the Secretary whether lists of national and other records are being printed in the programme, and whether *all* overseas competitors' national records are included. A good Meeting Secretary will provide this information. If a list is not being included in the programme, figures can be obtained from a local representative of the National Union of Track Statisticians or from the AAA Office. The figures should be kept with the programme. If a record is seen to be bettered or equalled, watches can then be examined. A note of when and where kilometre times are to be taken is also useful so the Chief can check that his teams are in position before the race is started. Organisers could help here by providing a plan of the track with the necessary timing positions marked (note that steeplechase kilometres are at odd places). Lap times and others may be written on the Timekeepers' Record Forms if special ones are not provided.

It will be necessary to have familiarised yourself with the arrangements needed for splits in the longer relay races in which bends are used. During the Briefing Meeting the Chief will see that the Timekeepers concerned know where the first take-over times have to be taken. The time for the baton to come to the line is taken for the splits, and the times should be written on the sheet provided; aggregate times will suffice. It saves possible confusion if the Timekeepers taking the team splits also time this team at the finish, but note that forethought is then needed with the team arrangement.

Sometimes there may be requests for team splits in $4 \times 100m$ or $4 \times 200m$ relays; don't be tempted! Such split team timings are for running starts and /or incorrect distances. Fond of them as Team Managers may be, such splits are inaccurate. Appeals for these, and for hand timings to hundredths (e.g. to resolve fastest loser problems – the Referee's province) must be resolutely refused and enquirers referred to the Rules: ' . . . hand times shall be rounded up to the next longer 1/10 second'.

AT THE MEETING

If all this preparatory work has been done well, the meeting itself should pose no new problems. In a less important meeting, however, there may be no Technical Committee Meeting before-hand and the Chief should then be at the meeting early enough to contact the Meeting Organiser, Referee, Chief Starter, Announcers, Photo-finish Chief and Clerk of the Course, in order to make all the necessary arrangements previously noted.

It is important that the Chief Timekeeper at a meeting should know the conditions by which competitors in heats proceed to the next round, for example the first in each heat and the two fastest losers, so that arrangements can be made – especially if there are fewer Timekeepers than really necessary – for an adequate number timing the placings concerned. This may demand rearrangement of the team for these heats. If the con-ditions are as stated above, the fastest losers may come from one heat, so it will be necessary to have sufficient Timekeepers on the second, third and possibly fourth positions. Good Seeding Officers will ensure that the Timekeepers know the conditions, and in good time to make any required adjustments to their team's duties. Such rearrangements are, of course, the Chief's responsibility; this is where timekeeping can influence the result of the competition.

When hand timing only is used, the duties of the Chief Time-keeper are defined in Rules 31, 40 and others, and in IAAF Rule 120. Photo-finish – the IAAF's 'fully automatic electrical timing' – is generally in use at major meetings, and it is import-ant that the Chief Timekeeper appreciates both his and the Photo-finish team's duties and responsibilities, defined in IAAF Rules and in the BAAB Code of Practice. The technical pro-duction of the photo-finish picture devolves on the Photo-finish team; it is not easy, and the Photo-finish Chief can well have more anxieties than the Chief Timekeeper.

It has been found good practice to include in the Photo-finish team a Timekeeper and a Track Judge (either of whom may be the Chief of the Photo-finish team) to assist with the reading of the photograph. They are responsible to the Chief Timekeeper and the Referee respectively, and, *in any case of doubt*, the picture must be seen by the Track Referee to decide placings, and by the Chief Timekeeper to decide times. Naturally, it will be a co-operative duty in most cases of very close finishes or records, for with applications for records the Track Referee has to certify that the placings, and times, are correct. At international meetings the President of the Jury of Appeal may also be invited to the 'viewing' – it may avoid problems later.

As noted earlier, the Chief Timekeeper may decide that the times from the photo-finish picture are inaccurate. In this case the hand times become official; this may be, for example, if the timing device was started manually instead of by automatic electrical means at the instant of the flash from the pistol charge. All such problems require, besides a full co-operation, mutual trust, respect and understanding, a speedy system of communication between the teams concerned - Starter, Track Referee, Chief Timekeeper and Photo-finish team. This will do much to aid the smooth presentation, and the cost of a radio link (walkie-talkie) would be a small price to pay for it.

Chief Timekeepers, for it is now their responsibility as well as that of the Referee, must ensure that the photo-finish film picture, and any part of it (for example a print from it) remains confidential to the Association's, Board's, or Federation's Officials of the meeting. After the meeting the Photo-finish team Chief will arrange for any reprocessing (for example rewashing) necessary to ensure permanence of the images. The film will then be sent to the appropriate authority for safe keeping.

With this modern concern of Chief Timekeepers with photo-finish timing, the more progressive will want to know at least how it works and how accurate it is. It is useful knowledge even if it only helps our understanding of some of the difficulties the Photo-finish team may encounter. It is suggested that all who take their timekeeping seriously should attend one of the courses on Photo-finish Camera Operating and Appreciation, held in the Areas.

With all the preliminary work completed, the timekeeping seems the easy part! During the meeting, you need to be continually aware of the importance of presentation; for example, you may be annoyed at someone thoughtlessly obscuring your view of the finish, but to shout loudly and angrily at the offender is, besides being unseemly, often ineffective. It generally fails to persuade him to move in time, and probably distracts other members of the team: don't do it. Remind the team that as experienced Timekeepers they should be able to cope with such difficulties; an error in estimating the finish plane position by 10cm (4in) represents only about 0.01 second in a sprint finish. The public will not be attracted to athletics if the meeting is presented in an amateurish way, for there are some very professional rivals for the public's interest. To be irresolute about a time and delay results will only vex the customers, who may well decide to stay at home in future and watch some television show free from these frustrations. Nevertheless, frustrations can occur for the timekeeping team, such as the Starter holding up a final for no apparent reason; this may well be caused by some television programme timing. Good communications with the meeting's main Officials enable the reason to be given, and this should be conveyed to the team.

If a record is thought to be broken or equalled, the Chief *must* examine the watches recording this or these times. He should, as a courtesy at least, ask the Track Referee if he wishes to see the watches, for he has to sign the record application form certifying that he is satisfied with the correctness of the details submitted – *including times*. Similarly, he will need to have lap times, and the number of the lap leader throughout the event concerned (Rule 62).

The Chief must get the best possible performances from each member of his team. How he does this will depend on his own experience and personality. The importance of being alert and concentrating on the start and finish, yet at the same time remaining relaxed, will have been learned during his earliest timekeeping days. The Chief will therefore ensure that anxieties are minimised, remembering that a less experienced Timekeeper, perhaps at his first international meeting, and possibly working with strangers in prestigious new surroundings, is quite liable to be too tense. Of course, the Chief may well have similar, even greater, anxieties himself; he probably has, but he must not let this show. An edgy Chief will only get an edgy team. So the Chief should put at their ease any strangers in his team on being introduced, seeing that they chat with older team members, and if they seem particularly shy, getting an experienced hand to look after them. He should make sure that they are visited during the meeting and given a word or two of encouragement.

If you are the Chief, never be arrogant or officious; don't be too pedantic; give reasons for any decisions you may have to take so that all the Timekeepers feel part of the team. Don't act as if the team members are novice pupils at a Timekeepers' Course and you are the autocratic Master; a loud, self-advertising 'Watches zeroed' is quite unnecessary – at least if one wasn't, it certainly will be the next time! Don't criticise, at least during the meeting. The Chief should take more than his share of any blame, less than his share of any credit. Remember the importance of having a relaxed and happy team, and that good morale seeps down from above rather than welling up from below.

After the final race, there may be record application forms to be completed, and it saves trouble if the necessary signatures are obtained while the Officials are still present. From the list of record performances previously prepared, any possible new records will be known, and from the team arrangement list will be seen the Timekeepers whose signatures are required. They should be asked to wait until the Meeting Organiser or Technical Manager brings the form for completion, unless, of course, he prefers to send them on later.

With the duties ended, it only remains for the Chief to thank the team for their co-operation – on whose behalf he himself has done a few hours behind-the-scenes work, but generally had a most interesting time. He should be attentive to comments and suggestions; it is often worth writing a note to the proposer after the matter has been thought over away from the involvements of the meeting.

Before leaving the stadium, the Chief Timekeeper should contact the Technical Manager, Announcers and Press Liaison Officials to make sure that they have all the times they need, for items like lap splits can easily be overlooked in the stress of the meeting. The Photo-finish team should also be visited, and any problems discussed, notes compared, etc. If all has gone well, the tired Chief may now relax.

PERSONAL REQUIREMENTS

It will have been seen from the above that Chief Timekeepers need a different set of skills from those used by Grade Is, for while the timekeeping has to be of this high standard, the other tasks, both before and during the meeting, present far greater challenges. It is for this reason that the appointment of Chief Timekeepers cannot follow automatically after the 'three years satisfactory experience in Grade I' quoted in the Handbook.

A Chief Timekeeper at a meeting does much more than just get the times; his duties start some days before the meeting, and end after it. However, it is during the meeting that all the preparatory work comes to fulfilment and the challenges of the situations that may arise can test all his knowledge, skills, experience – and character. We can all hope to improve our skills, as the character tests provide opportunities for developing any latent potentials. It is easier – much easier – to list the attributes needed than to acquire them; being only human, most of us are deficient in one or more of the following:

1. *Leadership*. The exercise of skills for getting the best performance from his team, that is, the ability to organise his team to best advantage, to exploit any special skills, to be attentive to the team's needs, sympathetic, and while tolerant of any short-comings, supporting them to the best of his ability.
2. *Wise Decision Making*. This can only come from knowledge and experience allied with innate sincerity and integrity.
3. *Affability*. He should have an amiable manner.
4. *Approachability*. He should be readily available to discuss problems with colleagues, with the Referee, Starter, Photo-finish Team Leader, Technical Manager of the Meeting, Meeting Organiser, Representatives of the media and so on.
5. *Unflappability*. He must never get flustered under stress.
6. *Acceptability*. He must be an easy person to get on with.
7. *Good-humour*. And with the ability to retain it during a long and perhaps difficult meeting.

It is perhaps no accident that for most of the above attributes, the words end in . . . ability, for this sums it all up.

5
Allocation of Duties

Specifying the duties of the members of a timekeeping team is a task similar to a Referee's preparation of Judges' duty allocation lists. Arrangements for national and international meetings differ in detail, as noted later. Because the duties to be covered depend on the programme, the number of Timekeepers available and other considerations, there can be no set procedure; for example, a match with only two runners per team requires few Timekeepers, while a National Championship may require a team of two dozen or more if all the timekeeping duties are to be adequately covered as required by the rules. The following notes are intended to help candidates answering the Time-keepers' Advanced Written Paper, which invariably includes a question on team arrangement, and this carries a good pro-portion of the total marks.

Because there can be no standard layout, the question is a test of the candidates' experience and skill in arranging a team to best advantage and complying with the requirements of Rules 40 and 62. The team arrangement given in the earlier publication *The Technique of Starting and Timekeeping* (1963 and 1977) was based on the older six-lane tracks, and the 1st/4th, 2nd/5th arrangement suggested there has generally given way to 1st/5th, 2nd/6th or 1st/6th, 2nd/7th layouts for the longer events. Remember that in sprints it is only possible to take one time reliably; to suggest taking two times in sprints may well get the candidate no marks for the entire question! The Written Test and Practice are treated separately.

WRITTEN TEST

On starting to prepare a team arrangement for the Written Test (or, indeed in practice) it is useful to start with the team members in grade order, with Chiefs and Grade Is heading the list to take leading times in case records may be involved. The Written Test candidate is usually given a list comprising so many Chiefs – A,B,C etc., so many Grade Is – H,I,J, etc., and so many Grade IIs. The candidate, generally assumed to be one of the Grade Is, may be asked to prepare a team arrangement list for, for example, Area Championships, with events such as 100m, 200m, 400m, 800m, 1,500m, 3,000m, steeplechase, 10,000m, and a six-team 4 × 400m relay.

It is useful to have at least a mental list of the duties to be covered.

1.   Races starting in lanes (usually up to 8 runners):
(a) Sprints, that is, up to 400m – three Timekeepers per runner if possible, each taking *one* time.
(b) Races from 400m up to and including 800m – as for sprints, but Timekeepers may take two times, so freeing some for lap calling etc.
2.   Longer (line start) races. Timekeepers take two times, but bear in mind the additional requirements, such as:
(a) Lap time recording – at the finish line, the time of the leader and his number are needed.
(b) Lap time calling – to runners at the start line *and* finish line if the team complement permits.
(c) Lap times to Announcers – via walkie-talkies or, with the Announcer's agreement, in the Announcer's box, but it is not easy to estimate the quarter and half-laps from there.
(d) Kilometre times (Rule 140); two or three Timekeepers are required.
(e) Running watch – times read to a Recorder for each finisher from a watch started from the gun flash; split times are only possible with well-spaced finishers, otherwise time to the next second as in road events.
(f) Possible extra duties such as 1,500m times in one mile races – three Timekeepers (at least) for possible records.
3.   Relays. As 1(a) above, but team lap splits need special planning consideration. Unless the lane draw is known, Timekeepers will be asked to take splits for the team starting in a particular lane. It saves confusion if they time this team at the finish as well.

Having the Timekeepers listed in grade order in a vertical column, and the various types of events horizontally, it seems logical then to complete the pattern of squares; this makes it easy for the candidate (and the Examiner) to check that each placing is covered (by looking vertically up the column) and that each Timekeeper is fully employed (by glancing across horizontally). The Examiner will expect to find all the duties covered to the limit of the number of Timekeepers available. Examiners should provide plenty of squared paper for the exercise; the first trial can usually be improved on and an eraser may save time initially. Fig 2 shows a table for Timekeepers A to T for a normal Written Test question. Note that this is not the only solution – it may not even be a good one, for example the times on the later placings taken by lap callers may be thought difficult, although their calling will have been completed well before the runners finish.

The sprints or races in lanes are done first. The Examiner will look to see that the available Timekeepers have been optimally deployed, expecting to see Chiefs and Grade Is on the leading positions (in case of records), but the lower grades on the later placings should have a higher grade Timekeeper, if possible, with them. The line start events seem easier since each Timekeeper can take two place times, but there are the extra duties enumerated above to be considered. Relays pose special problems if team lap splits are required; the candidate just has to rely on his ingenuity. The teams' total times should be taken by the higher grade Timekeepers in case of records, and it is good practice for those taking a team's lap splits to time that team at the finish; with the Judges' placings, their timings may be used with the place timings.

Sometimes there is a second part to the question asking for amendments in case some Timekeepers fail to arrive. There is no simple solution – some duties like adequate cover on kilometre times, the running watch check etc., may have to be sacrificed, as may duplication of team splits in relays. Note should be taken of where the Rule book says 'it is desirable' or 'should', rather than 'must'. A note giving reasons for your choice may be helpful; the Examiner will want to see that the candidate has used his now meagre resources to the best advantage. It is useful

GRADE		RACES IN LANES								LINE START RACES												RELAY – PLACE TIMES					
TK		1	2	3	4	5	6	7	8	1	2	3	4	5	6	7	8	9	10	11	12	1	2	3	4	5	6
F	1	1								1					1							1		1			
A	C	1								1					1							1		1			
B	C	1								1					1							1		1			
C	C		1								1					1							1		1		
D	C		1								1					1							1		1		
E	C			1								1					1						1		1		
G	1		1								1					1								1		1	
H	1			1								1					1							1		1	
I	1				1							1						1				Lap Splits: Lane 1					
J	1					1				Running Watch												2					
K	1						1			Kilometre Times												3					
L	1							1		Kilometre Times												4					
M	2											1					1					5					
N	2		1								1					1						6					
O	2			1							1					1						6					
P	2				1					Lap Call-Finish Line 1 1												5					
Q	2					1				Lap Call – Start Line												4					
R	2								1	Lap Call to Announcers 1												3					
S	3		1													1		1				2					
T	3			1	1					Running Watch												1					

Note: Timekeeper F represents the Timekeeper sitting the examination.

Fig 2   The layout of a typical examination 'squared paper' answer sheet.

to leave the original layout as far as possible, moving up the lower-graded Timekeepers to fill the gaps.

Some candidates may prefer merely to list the Timekeepers and write in their duties against their names. With experience this may take less time than the squares layout, but it is more difficult to check; the squares layout is also easier for the Examiner to check.

Candidates will see from the marks allotted to each question the relative importance of each, and it is well to apportion the time devoted to each accordingly. For example, out of 100 marks the Team Arrangement question may carry 30 marks, or, if a two-part question, 40 to 50 marks. A mental arithmetic exercise to allot adequate time from the total time allowed is worthwhile – and use *all* this period for checking a question that carries so many marks.

TEAM ARRANGEMENT

Having read the above, you may think that team arrangement in practice must be easier. It isn't.

At local meetings the Chief will probably know all the team personally and so be able to use individuals' attributes to advantage. He will also know that there are ranges of abilities within grades, and the knowledgeable Chief will be mindful of his colleagues' needs to gain experience necessary for their advancement. At meetings further afield he can approach Time-keeper friends in that locality for opinions and notes on any special skills available; notes on disabilities too may avoid embarrassment.

The plan used for the Advanced Written Test may be followed in principle, but now, instead of mere ciphers, these are real Timekeepers – different grades, different abilities, from various areas, old friends, strangers, some of long experience, some anxious ones at their first major meeting. You will know those who often work in your area and can put the more experienced to work with the less practised ones; it seems good, if it can be arranged, to put Timekeepers from different Areas to work together in order to get to know one another better. Strangers to the area should receive special consideration, being introduced to the older, more experienced, locals and, if possible, working with one. Ladies among the strangers warrant special regard – if possible working with a local lady member of the team. Your Area is 'host', the others are 'guests' and should be given pre-ferential treatment.

Away from the theoretical and imaginary problems of the Written Test, there can be such practical considerations as, for example, treating 8-up 800m races as lane start or sprint timings, and for 1500m events, which often develop into tactical races and bunched finishes, it may be useful to have some special arrangement, for example, sprint timings or a 1st/8th, 2nd/9th etc., scheme. An example for an Area meeting is given in Fig 3.

Name	Grade	Ref. Letter	Races in Lanes	1500 (800) m	Races over 1500m	4 × 100m Relay	4 × 400m Relay	Other Duties
H. Else	Ch.	Ch.	1	1	1–4	1	1	
D. Cross	1	A	1	1–7	1–4	1	1	
Y. Knott	Ch.	B	1	1–7	1–4	1	– S.la.1	
A. Wonder	1	C	2	2–8	2–5	2	2	Ar.
Q. Pidd	2	D	2	2–8	2–5	2	2	
V. Good	Ch.	E	2	2–8	2–5	2	– S.la.2	
B. Quick	1	F	3	3–9	3–6	3	3	Ar.
W. Winkle	2	G	3	3–9	3–6	3	3	
G. Gander	1	H	3	3–9	3–6	3	– S.la.3	
M. Bond	1	I	4	4–10	7–10	4	4	Ar.
H. Dickory	2	J	4	4–10	7–10	4	4	
M. Muffet	1	K	4	4–10	7–10	4	– S.la.4	
P. Billee	1	L	5	5–11	8–11	5	5	Ar.
J. Hack	2	M	5	5–11	8–11	5	5	
J. Hill	1	N	5	5–11	8–11	5	– S.la.5	
B. Slow	2	O	6	6–12	9–12	6	6	Ar.
S. Head	2	P	6	6–12	9–12	6	6	
D. York	1	Q	6	6–12	Ltf.	6	– S.la.6	
F. Tuck	2	R	7	7–13	Km.	7	7	Ar.
L. John	2	S	7	LtA.	9–12	7	7	
R. Hood	1	T	7	Ltr.	Ltr.	7	– S.la.7	
T. Piper	2	U	8	—	Rwc.	8	8	Ar.
H. Dumpty	3	V	8	Ltf.	13–15	8	8	
M. Dawe	2	W	A	—	Km.	A	– S.la.8	
J. Bull	3	X	8	Lts.	Lcs.	A	A	Ar. & S.la.8
S. Simon	3	Y	A	—	A.	A	A A	
F. Queen	3	Ż	A	Ltr.	Rwr.	8	A A	

Key

A. – Alternate (IAAF – Additional).

S.la.8 – Splits on team in lane 8 (or other lane number as indicated).

Ar. – Agree times and report to Chief Timekeeper.

LtA. – Lap times to Announcers.

Ltr. – Lap times, and number of leader, and record.

Ltf. – Call lap times to runners at finish line.

Lts. – Call lap times to runners at start line.

Km. – Take and record kilometre times.

Rwc. – Running watch – call to recorder.

Rwr. – Record times from running watch.

Note: The above is one of the many possible team arrangements; there are no set rules. There is, for instance, much in favour of 1st/5th, 2nd/6th, or 1st/6th, 2nd/7th arrangements – it is a matter of personal preference and making the best use of your resources.

Fig 3   Timekeepers' duties in a typical team arrangement.

At meetings away from home, the problems are even more difficult; you will have to rely on the opinions of Timekeeper colleagues in that locality as to whether X is a good Grade II, whether Y could cope with relay splits and so on. The typical practical team layout shown is a simplified squares form which could be photocopied for handing to each team member. Some Timekeepers keep a supply of suitable forms for completion as required; they are useful for last-minute alterations, for example using 'alternates' to do the duties of an unexpected absentee. The example given is taken from an Area Championships, and reference letters are given assuming that photo-finish timings will be available, that the hand timings are recorded, and that the Chief will issue the results to the team – *see*, for example, Appendix V on practical performance standards.

For those with photocopying facilities, one of the Time-keepers' Instruction Cards of the booklet can be filled in and handed to each member of the team.

Timekeeper's Instruction Card

Name . . . . Ref . . . .
Please take times as follows:
    Races in lanes . . . . ·
    Other races . . . . ·
    Special duties . . . . ·
    . . . . ·
    . . . .
You will be working with . . . .
                and . . . .
Thank you

               . . . .
                  (Chief Timekeeper)

Fig 4   The layout of a typical Timekeeper's instruction card.

ALLOCATION OF DUTIES

At some large and prolonged meetings, two teams of Time-keepers, working in shifts, may be appointed under one Chief Timekeeper and a Deputy. Before team arrangements can be completed there will have to be close pre-meeting collaboration between them. The Chief and his Deputy are each in charge of their sub-teams, taking race-to-race decisions etc., but questions of policy and details such as the checking and signing of record applications normally devolve upon the Chief. Division of duties will depend on many factors such as the location of the venue and the homes of the team members, their travel facilities etc., in addition to general team arrangement considerations.

The duration of shifts needs special attention. Experience suggests that timekeeping accuracy may start to fall after a couple of hours of intensive work, although this varies with individuals. On the other hand, some Timekeepers find that their first few timings on restarting after a rest period tend to be unreliable. The balance is probably in favour of short shifts up to two hours for the best team performance. Changes of shift during a busy meeting are best arranged when there may be a delay in the programme, for example before a Hurdles event. Alternatively, a larger than usual timekeeping team can be pro-vided whose members can deputise for anyone who wishes to leave for refreshment or a break. This needs careful planning to ensure that the most competent Timekeepers are present for, for example, fastest loser situations when timekeeping can influence the final result. Such planning is a challenge even to the better Chiefs.

A different approach from timing normal track events applies to cross country races, marathons and fell races, with their large fields. Times to the next longer full second are usually taken from a running watch, and good Recorders are as important as skilled Timekeepers. Timers with print-out facilities are especially useful in checking recordings. Practical hints on Timekeeping at these events are given in Chapter 2.

6
The Photo-finish

Early moving pictures were used to investigate running action. Developments by Goerz (1854–1923) led to a viable system and photo-finish and timing were used at the 1948 London Olympics. Modern cameras are sophisticated and their precision optics and engineering are reflected in the cost – several thousand pounds for a camera and accessories.

Knowledge of the basic principles of photo-finish is required for the Timekeepers' Advanced Written Examination, but practical use of the equipment is valuable too, and candidates are urged to attend a course on photo-finish; they are held in most Areas, and include setting up the camera and other equipment, taking film strips, and analysing them for the timings and placings; Starters and others could also benefit from such a course. Appendix IV has notes on photo-finish practice but they are no substitute for a practical course.

The principles can be understood by imagining that you are in a room overlooking a busy highway, but the curtains are drawn leaving only a narrow slit of window through which the road can be seen. A car towing a caravan passes. You cannot see this all together, but first you see the car's bonnet, then the rest of the car, then the caravan. You are quite sure what passed even though you did not see it all at once, for the picture was retained in your memory, even the colours of the car and caravan. In a photo-finish camera there is also a vertical strip of window, in this case a narrow slit only a few tenths of a millimetre wide, and instead of your memory there is a photographic film strip. To do what your memory does for you in the above sequence of events, the film behind the camera slit moves in the opposite direction to that of the moving object being filmed because the picture in cameras is reversed. If the film traverse rate is proportional to the speed of the movement which is being photographed (in the ratio 'lens to film' to 'lens to road') the pictures will be of normal proportions as they are built up in sequence while the objects cross the narrow strip that the camera 'sees'.

In practice, the field of view is only a few centimetres wide. The film travers introduces 'time', as your memory did, as the picture is built up. If the car headlamp passed at *exactly* 3 o'clock – 3hours 00minutes 00.00 seconds – the rear light of the caravan at 3hours 00minutes 00.68 seconds, and the built-up picture of the car and caravan occupied 68mm of film, it can be seen that each millimetre of film represents 0.01 seconds. We have, as it were, 'photographed time'. We could therefore determine by a millimetre scale just when parts of the car and caravan passed the reference line, that is, what the film saw through the slit. For example, the car's rear light may have passed 0.34 seconds after the headlamp, and the edge of the caravan window at 0.46 seconds, and so on. A uniform film traverse speed permits a linear time-scale to be printed on the film, usually from a digital timer display near one edge of the film strip. It is worth noting that film traverse speed is not very critical, for only the image in the slit is being photographed, and if the film traverse speed should be incorrect, while the picture's *proportions* will be wrong *the sequence and time-scale will be correct.*

When used in athletics, the photo-finish camera 'sees' through the slit only a two or three centimetre strip along the finish line (the edge nearer the start in accordance with the rules), and with the film moving it records a blur – the spread out image of the finish line. It is useful (and now usual) to have the intersections of the lane lines and finish line painted black, that is in 5cm squares, so that a correctly aligned camera will record continuous streaks (looking like lane lines) on the film; their absence, or absence in inner or outer lanes, indicates that the camera was *not* properly aligned, and the picture is of little value. When the first part of the leading runner, say a finger, crosses the plane of the finish line, this is recorded on the film, as are subsequent arrivals – hand, wrist, arm, shoulder, torso, etc., and thus a picture is built up, as was our mental picture of the car and caravan. So we have a permanent record of events in exact sequence as they occurred at the plane of the finish, and a time-scale from an LED display near the edge of the film can also be recorded. The timer is started by the Starter's gun, and therefore the zero on the time scale represents the signal from the Starter's

Fig 5 A photo-finish record – figures at the bottom indicate the time at which each runner crosses the finish plane.

gun – the start of the race.

The exposed film is developed and fixed, usually in the camera, and after a rinse in water can be examined while still wet. 'Reading' is generally done with magnifying or projecting equipment, and the positions and timings are determined by moving a cursor, which must be *exactly* perpendicular to the lane line images, to the leading part of the torso of the runner concerned. The time is read off from the scale photographed near the edge of the film. The photographs shown are enlargements from photo-finish films of actual races: the vertical marks on Fig 5 are hundredths of a second introduced via the lens as the film is taken; Fig 6, with a close sprint finish, shows what skill and practice are needed to read the result. The difficulty with runners masking one another may be avoided by using a camera on each side of the track, or by a mirror system. Appendix IV has further notes. It must be stressed that photo-finish pictures are *confidential information* – *see* the Handbook, *Photo-finish – Code of Practice*.

Fig 6 In a close finish involving several runners, the photo-finish record plays a vital role in determining the winner.

This is the 'fully automatic timing' of IAAF Rule 120. Other methods, such as breaking light beams are *not* acceptable; the beams can be broken by hand and need not wait for a torso to come to the plane of the finish. No more authentic is video recording, for the horizontal scanning introduces a time-difference from top to bottom of the picture. There is, however, the possibility that vertical scanning at an appropriate frequency could provide the time resolution required, offering too the advantages of video recording and reproduction, such as instant play-back, image intensification, detail enlargement, transmission to multiple outlets, etc. This is the obvious way that photo-finish will progress. A prototype unit (1986) suggested exciting possibilities.

Appendix I

HOME PRACTICE

The following exercises will help you to achieve consistency of reactions.

1. *Pendulum.* The 1963 booklet's 'pendulum method' is probably the best for home practice because the angular speed of the bob approaching the door edge is not very different from that at which runners approach the finish line across your field of view. It would be hard to better Harry Hathway's description, reproduced below and 'metricated' here and there.

'A length of thread tied to the bob is passed between two pieces of plywood with edges trimmed straight. They are clamped together with their lower edges touching and horizontal, and the whole is fastened firmly to a rigid support so that the thread hangs close to a vertical edge such as an open door. The clamp screw is slackened and the length is adjusted until the centre of the bob is 224cm below the plywood edges. If the pendulum is now made to swing through about 5 degrees either side of the vertical (i.e. a distance of some 20cm on either side of the central point of its path) it will take approximately 1.5 seconds to swing from side to side. It should be timed with the stop-watch for 100 swings and the length adjusted until the time of 100 swings is 150 seconds, the clamp screw being slackened whenever the length has to be altered. A decrease of 1 per cent in the time is obtained by a reduction of 2 per cent in the length, and an increase of 1 second in the time of 100 swings is obtained by increasing the length by about 3cm.

'The timekeeper now stands in a position from which he can see the bob for exactly half of each swing, for example the arc BC (*see* Fig 7) of the total swing ABC. He starts his watch as soon as the bob appears at B, waits while it swings from B to C

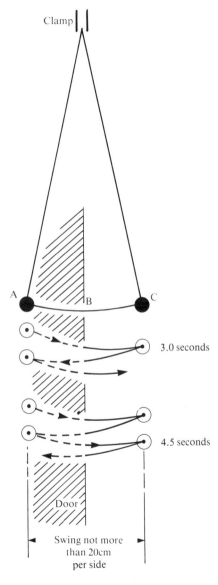

Clamp

A
B
C

3.0 seconds

4.5 seconds

Door

Swing not more
than 20cm
per side

Fig 7   Pendulum practice.

to B to A to B, and stops his watch as soon as the bob appears again. The time shown should be 3.0 seconds precisely.

'The timekeeper should continue with this exercise until he is getting the true time about 9 times in 10. He has then acquired a uniform reaction to an unexpected signal such as that reached at the start of a race. His next exercise is to start the watch as the bob appears at B, let it swing from B to C to B to A to B to C and to stop the watch as soon as the bob disappears at B. The time shown should be 4.5 seconds. It will in all probability be less than this and the deficit is due to anticipation of a signal which can be seen approaching, as can the signal at the finish of a race.'

An alternative 1 second pendulum with a length of about 99cm was also given – bob appearing, 2 seconds; bob disappearing, 3 seconds. A precaution hinted at in the original text might be noted: do not practise for too long at one session, because after a few dozen timings, it seems only too easy to estimate – and fairly accurately too – just when the bob will appear or disappear. The 'pendulum method' has certainly proved splendid practice; it is especially recommended before a Practical Test.

2. *Digital read-out timer.* The self-measurement of reaction time described in the earlier booklet using a cover on the dial of a stop-watch calibrated in hundredths is still valid – if a suitable watch can be found. Using an electronic timer with digital read-out for the exercise can be done with opaque tape covering the unit seconds, the tenths and hundredths. The timer is started and the 'tens' of seconds watched. When the 1 appears, i.e., at the change from 9.99 to 10.00 seconds, the timer is stopped, the plastic strip peeled back and the time delay read, perhaps 0.00′ 10.18, a reaction time of 0.18 seconds. Although the time taken in the test is longer than with the 3-second dial stop-watch of the earlier booklet, it has the advantage that there is less chance of subconsciously memorising the shorter time.

3. *Falling dart.* A falling body may be used, for example a dart with a tail carrying the calibrations. The dart can be made from a strip of stiff card some 3 or 4cm wide; it can be tapered towards the tail, which can be folded out to aid stability, and the 'zero' end weighted with a paper clip and adhesive tape.

Accuracy is not essential even in the calibration, for the

'pointer' is only a finger and thumb. The calibrations are measured from the weighted end of the dart as follows:

0		0.10	0.12	0.15	0.17	0.20	0.22 seconds
end of dart		5	7	11	14	20	24cm from end of dart

Fig 8, to about one-third scale, will give an idea of the general appearance.

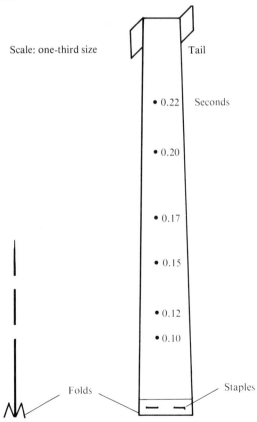

Scale: one-third size

Tail

• 0.22 Seconds

• 0.20

• 0.17

• 0.15

• 0.12

• 0.10

Folds

Staples

Fig 8 A paper dart to measure reaction times.

Two players use the dart, A and B. A holds the dart near its tail, letting it hang vertically while B holds a finger and thumb a few centimetres apart, *but not touching the dart*, at the zero end. The dart is suddenly released by A and stopped by B closing his thumb and finger. This will indicate the time taken to get finger movement from a sudden, unexpected signal. A few trials will demonstrate that it really does take so long to react. The players then change over, when A finds that he too has slow reactions! Cheating by following the dart with the fingers can be avoided by having the victim rest his elbow on the table.

From the 'pendulum practice' and other tests it soon becomes clear that although we may be good Timekeepers with similar signals (that is, from the appearance, disappearance and then reappearance of the bob, when we all get close to the pendulum period), we do not do so well when we time the interval to the *disappearance* of the bob; too often, alas, we are a tenth of a second or more fast. We have to unlearn the anticipation required in tasks like catching moving objects. Appendix II has some notes on the physiology.

Another belief may come into question as experience with the test is gained – that concerning your personal reaction time. We all believe that ours is phenomenally fast; it isn't. The time taken from seeing a signal (the flash from the Starter's gun, or the bob appearing from behind the door) to the point when the finger can operate a timer push-piece approaches two-tenths of a second. Lamentable as this may be when we are dealing in hundredths of a second, it really is a built-in fact of life. Never-the-less, to Timekeepers *the delay is unimportant if it is consistent at start and finish*.

Appendix II

REACTION TIMES

The physiology involved in reaction times is interesting enough to warrant a note, although it is not required for the Written Paper. The signal from the Starter's gun takes a very short time indeed to reach our eyes. We then have to 'see it', that is, the signal at the retina must be sent via nerves to the brain. Nerves transmit impulses by some complex chemical and electrical effects. Time is required for the electro-chemistry, and the speed of signals' transmission via nerves is around a few metres per second, although this varies with the type of nerves involved.

In probably a few hundredths of a second the visual signal from the flash will have traversed the short distance from eye to brain; we see the signal. The brain then commissions longer nerves down an arm to a finger and orders it to start the watch. This accounts for most of the delay unavoidably incurred.

Physiologists have studied the effect of strong and weak signals (light flashes, sound and touch) on reaction time delay, which is important in modern technology when there happens to be some human component in an otherwise automatically controlled system. The first hint of a reaction time delay in relation to timekeeping came from a report on some astronomical data discrepancies from the Royal Observatory in 1799 on the timing of star transits – no doubt due to anticipation. We are still indebted to the Royal Observatory for our accurate time.

With this built-in delay, how do we manage to do anything precisely? We use anticipation. Dancers anticipate the beat before they hear it. Such rhythmic signals present few problems, but it is a little more difficult when we have to hit moving targets or catch anything moving. However, we learn to do such things early in life and, using anticipation, can generally achieve a reaction time of 0.05 seconds or less. In timekeeping anticipation must *not* be used; we have to unlearn some lifelong habits.

Appendix III

PRACTICAL TESTS

These notes on Practical Tests for Timekeepers using digital timers are issued by the Combined Officials' Committee.

ORGANISATION OF TEST

The County, District, Service, etc., having six or more candidates, will request the Area Officials' Secretary to arrange the Test, that is, to select a date, time and venue when:

1. A Chief Timekeeper is available to act as Master.
2. A Starter is available with a .38 or .45 pistol and ammunition known to give a satisfactory flash.
3. A dozen or more athletes can be present to run the races.
4. A well-defined track has been prepared with posts and a properly marked finish line (lanes are not necessary).
5. Stands are available for the candidates and Recorders at the finish.

Note that a photo-finish camera is an ideal but costly Master. However, it may be possible to combine a Timekeepers' Practical Test with a photo-finish course to minimise expenses. A Master is still required for administration.

Multiple-beam photo cell equipment, with logic circuits to avoid difficulties with leading hands or arms, may provide useful back-up for a Master. They are not as accurate as photo-finish records, but are of some value.

In the past Timekeepers' Practicals have been held in conjunction with sports meetings at which sufficient sprints are run. This practice is deprecated as possibly unfair to candidates as there are likely to be distractions.

NOTICE OF TEST

On completion of the above arrangements – perhaps two or three weeks before the date of the Test, the local County or District Secretaries and Officials' Secretaries should be notified so that invitations can be sent telling prospective candidates of the time and place of the Test. They should be asked to arrive at the venue half an hour before the Test is due to start, to bring a reliable timer reading in hundredths, a friend to act as Recorder (a graded Timekeeper is ideal), and the Test fee. It is useful to advise candidates that the Test should take about an hour and a half to two hours given good co-operation from the athletes and efficient marshalling. Note that neighbouring counties may also be invited at the discretion of the host County's Officials' Secretary.

PRINCIPLES OF THE TEST

1. *Fairness*. The objectives throughout the Test must be to see that all the conditions are fair, even helpful, to the candidates. Some may well be nervous (not conducive to good timekeeping performances) so the Master should try to put them at their ease and explain how the Test will be conducted to give them the best possible chance of getting good marks. There will be some forty races to time, but no race will be started until everyone is ready, they will only have to time the firsts each time, and the marks allow for a fair margin of error.

2. *The Master's duties*. As the candidates are arriving, their timers should be checked to ensure that there are no significant starting, stopping or display faults. The track, finish line, and posts are inspected and the stands put in the required position, *never* closer than 6m to the nearest lane and better 10m or more from it. Candidates should be in single line if numbers permit this; if not, the Master should satisfy himself that candidates, particularly at the front of the stand, have a good line of sight to the finish plane and the Starter. Recorders should have good access to the candidates – this saves time. With the candidates assembled it is useful to remind them of the conditions of the

Test; *no* talking, and how the times are taken from the flash of the gun to the torso of the runner interrupting their view of the plane of the finish (the far post, in practice), when they will start to stop the timer. The Recorder notes the times they have. In practice, one Recorder can write down the times of two candidates with little loss of time.

3. *The Recorders.* The value of the Recorders is explained: they are there to avoid divulging the candidates' times since these may be disconcerting to other candidates. The Master should make sure that the Recorders have no difficulty in reading the timers correctly, that they each have the necessary form with their candidates' reference number on it, and are reminded, in case of difficulty in reading the times, or any disagreement with the candidate about the time recorded for any race, that the Recorder must take the timer and record sheet to the Master who will decide on the time to be recorded.

4. *Recording.* The Recorders will read the time from the candidate's timer for each race and write it down clearly against the race number on the form provided. The times registered in hundredths will be recorded. The time written down will be shown to the candidate for confirmation. If the candidate disagrees with the time recorded, without saying anything the Recorder will take the timer and the record sheet to the Master who will read the candidate's timer and enter, and initial, the time on the record form. If the timer should have developed a fault (e.g., display incomplete) the timer should be changed – the Master usefully carries spares – and that result disregarded.

PRELIMINARIES

With the candidates and Recorders assembled on the stands, the Master should remind the candidates and Recorders of the procedure and the reasons for it. It is then useful to have two or three trial races (no more, or some candidates may lose concentration later) to make sure that the Recorders are reading the timers correctly, and that candidates have a good view of the Starter's pistol. After each of these trial races the Master can tell each candidate his time and say how easy it all is. 'I had 13.33, so 13.23 to 13.43 will count as correct'. These trial races are helpful in putting candidates at their ease and ensuring that there is a satisfactory background for the Starter's flash – he should be asked to move if a better background seems available, for he does not have to control the start. The opportunity should also be taken to ask candidates if they can foresee any difficulty; this is the time to try to remedy it.

RACES

Forty races are about the best number – fewer may be unfair if a candidate takes time to settle down, or misses one or two, and more races may result in some candidates losing concentration. It is useful for the Master to talk to the runners before the start of the Test, telling them what is going on, that there will be no false starts or recalls, that they need not run the whole distance, but please hurry and make it look like a race over the final few metres. A Starter's Assistant/Competitors' Marshall is a big help and can save a lot of time.

THE START

While the Starter should be about 80 to 100 metres from the candidates – and for several races even further away to ascertain that the candidates react quickly to a weaker stimulus – the runners can start nearer the finish if they wish. Coaches often like to avail themselves of so much starting practice and sprint coaching, so may get the runners to start properly and run the full distance. The Starter, having the runners assembled – a minimum of three per race is suggested – will follow the standard AAA Competition procedure of blowing a whistle to ascertain that the Timekeepers are ready. At this signal the Master will ensure that *all* the candidates are ready (perhaps reminding them to zero their timers) and then signal to the Starter to proceed. He will raise the gun vertically to arms' length, and if it has a stopped barrel will make sure that the side hole is facing the candidates. He fires.

THE FINISH

A white line 5cm wide at right angles to the track with vertical posts 30cm or so outside the track must be provided as in the Rules. The candidates, on their elevated stands, must each have a clear view of this. Both sides of the track may be used. The Master generally stands at ground level for convenience of consultation with the candidates/Recorders, the Starter and others. He may, if he so wishes, record his own times. If there should be so many candidates that stands are needed inside and outside the track, the Master should take times from near each of the stands so that neither side seems to be unduly favoured.

MARKING

Candidates' times which are not more than 0.10 second different from the Master's times will be marked correct.

COMPLETION OF TEST

The organiser will collect the candidates' and the Master's records for the Marker appointed by the Area Officials' Committee. When marked as in the previous paragraph, the candidates will be notified of the percentage marks they obtained – percentages rounded to the nearest one per cent.

It is kind to the candidates, if time permits, for the Master to look through the times recorded by the candidates in comparison with his own times record and give a *rough assessment* of each candidate's performance. The Master must explain that these marks are *unofficial* and *very approximate indeed*. (He will naturally err on the pessimistic side if in doubt.) But it is useful to the candidates, and saves them waiting on tenter-hooks for a week or two.

Finally, the Master should thank the Starter, local Club Officials, athletes, Marshalls and Recorders for their help.

Appendix IV

PHOTO-FINISH PRACTICE

Mere notes cannot be any substitute for practice and serious Timekeepers are therefore urged to attend a course, offered in most areas, on photo-finish appreciation, and demonstrating how their contributions can be co-ordinated for the better presentation of athletics.

The principles have been outlined in Chapter 6; they are realised in different ways in the various camera systems and operations are consequently so varied that practice with them is necessary. However, some broad essentials can be noted which may serve as an introduction to the practical course earnestly recommended.

1. *Optical considerations*. These require the image of the finish line to be focused on to the film which is just behind (in contact with) the slit. To minimise the possibility of runners masking one another, the camera needs to be in an elevated position exactly in line with the finish and sufficiently remote to cover all the lanes plus the height of the runners. Ideally, *two* cameras on opposite sides of the track – or a mirror system as used in horse racing – can be used to avoid masking. There is no best distance, or best height, and no best angle, but between about 10 degrees and 30 degrees to the horizontal is usual and this range covers most situations with the runners generally from 10 to 40 metres from the camera. 'Zoom' lenses have superseded exercises in trigonometry to find the focal length required and the almost standard 80 to 250mm zoom will deal with most situations; about 150mm is usual for most fixed site cameras.

The camera is set up on its mountings (sometimes a tripod, but this must be a very rigid one, and even so sand bags around each leg are useful) and roughly aligned by eye. With the camera lens in place, an image of the track can be observed through an eye-piece via a mirror system (which can be interposed by a control knob) in the path of the image to the slit.

The zoom can be adjusted for the required track coverage and focused for best sharpness so that the camera can then be accurately aligned. The lens should be at full aperture to give a sufficiently bright image of the track. (Some simpler cameras have a telescope or 'sighting tube' instead of the mirror system). Vertical alignment and picture size must cover from the lane nearest the camera to the farthest lane including a tall runner, and horizontally the viewfinder cursor should be accurately on the nearer edge of the finish line to the start (remember that the image is reversed; the lane numbers on the track are usually 'nearer the start'). After a final check the mountings are tightened and any wedges used are placed in position; then *recheck*. The viewing mirror, on cameras so provided, must be returned, or there will be no picture!

2. *Photographic and processing requirements*. These are rather special. Continuous film systems use fine-grain film on a special base formulated for processing at high temperatures. Alternatively, for example with Accutrack cameras, the Polaroid system's very fast emulsion on paper sheet backing is used. The in-package processing is complete in about 15 seconds after pulling the pack from its holder, after which the backing paper can be peeled away and the picture examined. Copies require other equipment and cannot normally be carried out on site.

A typical continuous film camera, the Omega OPS-2, has a processing unit attached to the camera and it is arranged that the exposed film is pulled through the developer and fixer in their separate compartments at a predetermined speed to give the required processing times. Alternatively, or in other cameras, the film may be processed away from the camera in a dark room or transferred in a special cassette to a lightproof 'glove box' in which the developing and fixing are done by time and temperature techniques. Washing to remove the processing chemicals by a quick rinse in clean water is adequate for on-site viewing, but for permanence the film should be rewashed for at least half an hour in running water.

Processing chemicals are made up from concentrates. Developer is usually in two packets of powders and the instructions on the package must be followed implicitly.

The powders contain strong alkalis (which harm skin and stain clothing, so splashes should be avoided or a protective overall worn) and metol, which may cause irritation to some sensitive skins, so frequent rinsing of the hands in clean water is recommended. Next to the camera, buckets of water are essential, if inelegant, adjuncts to the equipment. Fixer concentrate liquid merely needs dilution with usually twice its volume of water. It saves time if hand warm (perhaps 40 degrees Celsius) water can be obtained to facilitate dissolution of the developer chemicals – which should be added slowly, with continuous stirring, or they tend to coalesce into awkward lumps. Warm water also saves heating time when the processor unit is connected to its electrical supply to maintain the required temperature. Volumes of processing chemicals required depend on the system used – typically, for the Omega OPS-2, 600ml of developer and fixer will process the standard 150ft of film before renewal (enough for an averagely long meeting).

Film loading should be done, but never in direct sunlight, to the camera maker's instructions. The dull (emulsion) side of the film should be nearest the slit, and if pressure pads are provided they must be locked in position after all has been checked: light-proof covers are then placed in position and secured. While the above is being done, a colleague should be checking the off camera equipment.

3. *Ancillary equipment.* This includes electrical supplies, gun-lines to the various start positions, communication links, and viewing apparatus amongst other things, and can be checked while processing chemicals are being made up and the camera loaded. Difficulties are often met with gun-lines and their connections so checking them is an important duty; systems vary and details can only be learned by practice. It is a job for two people – one at the camera to watch indicators (meters and/or lights), and one to go to each start position to plug in the pistol, transducer, or dummy lead and switch as required, and to signal, for example by whistle, to the camera site when a trial is to be made. If all is well at the camera, a signal, or whistle or flag, will indicate this. If there are problems not resolved by common-sense checking for loose connections, etc., it may be necessary to

seek the stadium staff's help. Untoward difficulties can take time to correct – hence the need for Photo-finish team to be on duty early, say two hours before the first race. When all the gun-lines have been proved satisfactory, a trial film should be made. Competitors warming up can be used for practice and the film examined. If all is well the lane lines (from the back squares at lane and finish line intersections) will all be present, the runners well defined and the time-scale clear.

4. *Operating difficulties*. Sometimes the trial run may reveal that all is *not* well and then a logical approach can minimise anxiety and save time – it is for this reason that the principles should be well understood and some practical experience gained under a practised operator of photo-finish equipment. Problems, for example, may include:

(a) No picture, *nor time-scale*, and the film black – it may have been exposed to light during loading (it is difficult to avoid exposing the first metre or so of film). If clear film does not emerge after a few metres have been processed, a camera cover may be insecure or the film may be faulty. Sometimes an alternative position for the processing unit (for example on the Omega OPS-2) permits operation by either hand; the unused hole must be closed by the plug provided to avoid light ingress.

If the film is grey/white, the processor tank may be cold, the developer faulty (old stock), the chemicals in wrong compartments in the tank or mutually contaminated, for example by an unsteady camera.

If the film is black and warped, the processor tank is too hot, possibly caused by a thermostat fault.

(b) No picture, but time-scale clear. In this case, the viewing mirror may not have been returned, there may be a cover on the lens, or other obstruction, or a gross error in exposure – the lens aperture should be checked.

(c) Picture is present, but poor, and the time-scale is clear. In this case, if the picture is fuzzy, check the focus. If it is milky white, with a faint time-scale, cold processing, spoiled or used fixer may be the cause. Try refixing in stock solution as soon as possible.

If the picture is the wrong size, check the zoom (the camera may then need realignment). If the runners are satisfactory, but lane-lines are missing, alignment is incorrect.

A picture with irregular vertical streaks shows that the film is not being pulled correctly – check that it is secure on the pulling roller.

A picture with *regular* vertical streaks is produced in alternating current lighting with gas-discharge lamps which give strobe effects. (Multi-phase connections will minimise this problem, but it is not a quick DIY job).

A picture with horizontal streaks suggests that there is dust in the slit. On cameras with adjustable slits (for example Omega OPS models), opening and closing the slit may dislodge the dust particle. Otherwise remove the dust with a camel-hair brush or *soft* tissue; anything harder, even a paper towel, may do costly damage.

Irregular patterns, like trees, can be caused by electro-static charges built up in a dry atmosphere. They are rare, but puzzling, and usually the result of film storage at too high a temperature. Film stocks, in sealed containers, can be stored in refrigerators at 2 to 10 degrees Celsius. A walnut-sized wad of moist tissue wedged in a spare corner of the film traverse compartment has been found to minimise this effect by increasing local humidity.

(d) Streaks and irregular time-scale – *see* (c) above, otherwise supply voltage may be low or the connection intermittent.

(e) During a meeting with all the photo-finish operations going well, there may be, from some unnoticed cause, a failure of the camera timer to start. For instance, a gun line may have been left connected at another start position (the lines are in parallel and the circuit has to be *broken*). The camera timer must be started by hand; the pictures will be in their correct sequence and so of value to Judges, and while the times will be wrong the intervals will be correct. It is good practice in this situation to delay the manual start until the leader has only some 50 metres to run thus giving an obviously wrong timing. The result slip must be marked *manual start* and the Chief Timekeeper advised immediately: the official timings will then be hand times, i.e. to one tenth of a second.

5. *Viewing*. The rinsed film, with excess water removed by sliding through fingers, can be viewed immediately by placing it

in a glass slide (to which it adheres by surface tension) in an enlarger/viewer and aligning the picture to a cursor line exactly perpendicular to the lane-lines (and time-scale). The glass slide and film are moved along to align the torso and times. Reading the film is normally a two-person job – one should be a Judge, the other a Timekeeper, one reading, the other checking and recording on the result slip which is sent to the Results Co-ordinator, Announcers, and other officials. Some practice is needed, especially if runners in a blanket finish mask one another; again, attendance on a Course is essential for practice in resolving these problems.

Remember that the films are confidential information, not for public viewing, or for the media, and may only be seen by the meeting's officials and Jury of Appeal members and are then kept secure. After the meeting the films should be rewashed, dried, and sent to the meeting's governing body for safe keeping. Prints will be required to accompany claims for records.

Areas hold Photo-finish Appreciation Courses when the principles of photo-finish are demonstrated, the camera and its controls examined, ancillary equipment explained, and practice at reading the film is given. Dedicated Timekeepers are urged to attend such a session, and Judges, Starters and Marksmen can also benefit.

Appendix V

ASSESSMENT OF PERSONAL PERFORMANCE

Records of your performance against photo-finish timings form a useful commentary on personal timekeeping accuracy. Two factors, found by simple arithmetic, are required: the average error and an index for the spread. To record only the average error is hardly worth doing. A very poor Timekeeper getting the wildest results could, by chance, have his awful 'fast' and 'slow' timings cancel each other out and come to an average of nearly zero; on the other hand, a much better Timekeeper, generally getting within a few hundredths of the photo-finish times, may have an average error of 2 or 3 hundredths off zero, but with a total spread of, say 10 hundredths. To assess the standard of our timekeeping requires what the statisticians refer to as a mean (which we may take to be an average) and an index of spread which they call standard deviation, denoted by the Greek small letter sigma in textbooks and on some calculators. Timekeepers familiar with these concepts can do their own calculations, or get their pocket calculators to do them for them, but a good enough estimate of the index of spread can be determined by noting the extremes of the spread (the statisticians' range) and dividing by a factor related to the number of timings. Note that the factors given here are approximate and there is no reliable factor for fewer than ten timings.

Number of Timings:	1–9	10–19	20–29	30–39	40–69	70–199	200 +
Divide by:	–	$3^{1}/_{3}$	$3^{1}/_{2}$	4	$4^{1}/_{2}$	5	6

For example, if for 24 timings a Timekeeper's worst errors were 0.07 seconds fast and 0.05 seconds slow, there is a total spread of 0.12 seconds and the factor for 20–29 races is $3\frac{1}{2}$. Dividing 0.12 by 3.5 gives about 0.035 for our Index of Spread, which is not far from the statisticians' Standard Deviation in most examples of timekeeping errors. The other factor, the average, is easily worked out, or if we are very idle and acknowledge that the arithmetic is very rough and ready, it will in most cases be adequate to take the middle of the extremes of the spread. In our example then, the average may be taken as 0.01 seconds fast. These are the two factors required; although very approximate, they are much better than our own generally flattering recollections of accurate timings. When a lot of comparisons can be made, these are likely to give more reliable estimates than when only a few comparisons are possible and it may be useful to note the number of timings compared.

Keeping records of these two figures throughout a season, and season by season, gives a useful measure of our performances and is a much more reliable guide than remembering the times only when you exactly agreed with the photo-finish times, and forgetting the bad ones. Fig 9 shows a typical record.

	Date	Meeting	No. of Timings	Hundredths of seconds Slow–Fast						Hundredths of seconds Standard Deviation			
				3	2	1	1	2	3	1	2	3	4
1985	15–26 Jan.	AAA	43			•					•		
	9 Mar.	vUSA	15				•				•		
	15–16 Mar.	Under 20	34					•			•		
	8–9 June	Eur.Cup	47		•						•		
	4 Aug.	BAL	22	•						•			
1986	24–25 Jan.	WAAA	88	•							•		
	8 Feb.	vHungary	15		•						•		
	8 Mar.	vUSA	12				•			•			
	31 May	BAL	31				•				•		
	7–8 June	Decathlon	27			•						•	
	20–21 June	AAA	35		•						•		
	17 Aug.	Relays	19				•				•		

Fig 9   A typical Timekeeper's performance chart.

Event no.		7	8	9	11	12	13	15	16
Race		400m Hurdles	100m	800m	3000m	200m Women	400m	3000m Steeple-chase	110m Hurdles
TK									
Place 1st	D	50.35	10.(34)	1-46.96	8-00.63	22.71	46.(88)	8-34.70	13.31.
	W	.(34)	.32	.(92)	.(70)	.70	.92	.(62)	.(42)
	Z	.(33)	.38	.94	.(67)	.(75)	.(91)	.(61)	.38
	P-f	50.32	10.35	1-46.91	8-00.68	22.74	46.89	8-34.63	13.41
2nd	E	50.(46)	10.32	1-47.(03)	8-01.(88)	23.26	47.(20)	8-37.(76)	13.(57)
	P	.57	.33	.04	.(87)	.(29)	.(21)	.86	.49
	X	.(46)	.30	.96	.80	.26	.18	.75	.47
	P-f	50.46	10.36	1-47.01	8-01.87	23.29	47.21	8-37.78	13.57
3rd	H	51.06	10.48	1-47.08	8-03.03	23.28	47.(50)	8-40.14	13.(59)
	N	.08	.(38)	.22	.97	.27	.(50)	.(08)	.56
	Q	.(03)	.30	.13	.(14)	.30	.(53)	.(05)	.54
	P-f	51.01	10.40	1-47.17	8-03.15	23.34	47.51	8-40.07	13.61

Note: TK column shows the Timekeepers' reference letters. P-f denotes photo-finish time and rings mark times within 0.02 seconds of the photo-finish timing.

Fig 10   Timekeepers' performances for a meeting between England, Hungary and Poland.

Chief Timekeepers at international meetings will have their team's signed record forms, and I believe it is helpful, as well as interesting, for team members to be issued with a table of the team's timings, together with the photo-finish times. It is for such tables that the Reference Letter is used, so some degree of anonymity is preserved. Part of such a table appears in Fig 10. The ones that I issue are ringed for timings within 0.02 seconds of the photo-finish time – as near as hand times are likely to be. It is felt that such information provides a stimulus towards improving our timing performances and that the modest effort required is very worthwhile. Performances like those of E, W and Z in the table are commendable, and, no doubt, the outcome of long practice of the timekeeping arts. They indicate what can be achieved with dedication. To misquote Dr Johnson: 'What we hope ever to do with ease, we must first practise with diligence'. It could well be a motto for Timekeepers.